WALRUSSEY

BEX HAINSWORTH

Black Cat Poetry Press

Editor: Satya Bosman
Artist Design: Lucia Bosman
www.blackcatpress.co.uk

Copyright © 2023

All rights reserved. No part of this book may be reproduced in any manner whatsoever without written permission of the authors except in the case of reprints in the context of reviews.

Cover art design by Lucia Bosman
ISBN: 9781739781156

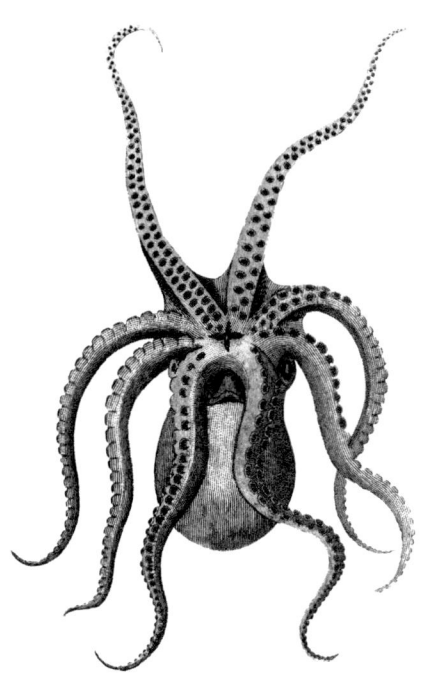

For Sam

Contents

09	An Octopus Picks Litter at the End of the World
10	Fin
11	Beluga
12	Whale Fall
14	Lobsters
15	Bucca
16	Hatchlings
18	Valley of the Whales
19	Bleaching
20	Floodplain
21	Two Whale Sharks Collide at the Aquarium
22	Goose Barnacles
23	Early Morning Manatee
24	Greenland Shark
25	Jellyfish
27	Ghosting
28	The Loneliness of the Long Distance Waddler
29	Consider the Selkie
30	Sand Tiger Sharks at the Frying Pan Tower
31	Tide Pool
32	My Father Eating Mussels
33	Thresher Shark
34	Walrussey
35	Mola mola
37	Lion's Mane Jellyfish
39	Ichthyosaur Fossil at the Natural History Museum
40	Requiem for a Great White Shark in Formaldehyde
42	Blue Lobster

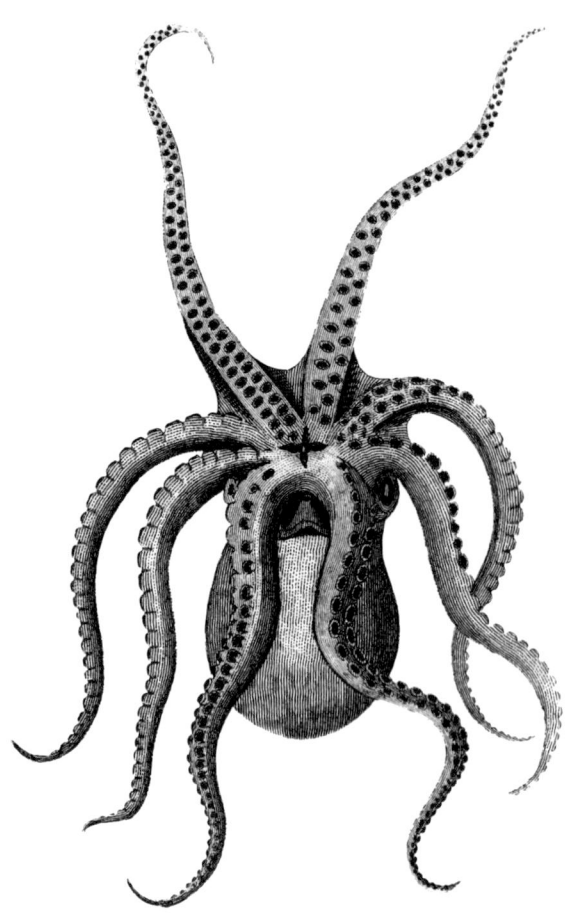

An Octopus Picks Litter at the End of the World

A serrated bottle cap. A triangle of green glass.
These are unusual shells: strange, immortal tools
that she collects during a morning's foraging.
The ring pull from a tin can slides over one tentacle tip
like the closing of a trap, but still she swims onwards,
a chameleon umbrella, shimmering like an oil spill.

She adapts. This alien debris has bewildered her
fellow sand-dwellers, but she is an architect, a pioneer.
A cave of can. An inverted volleyball is an ample bowl.
Yet she is also a soothsayer, a creature of Cassandra.
She senses the prickle of warmer water, the stirrings
of a terrible future. The sky is already falling around her.

A kinder death awaits. She is beginning to mimic
the gentle bloating of plastic bags across the blue.
Soon, she will retire to the darkness of a car tyre,
its black, fraying edges floating like a shroud.
Swelling with eggs, she will guard her nest:
starving artist, sacrifice, prophet-martyr.

Fin

A small mountain rises from the swell
beyond the bow. Grey-black, sleek
sheet metal, ready to be scrapped for parts.

The hammerhead is hauled onto the deck.
A silver hook of fear, pulsing, panicked,
twisting like an exposed muscle.

Pinned down, she is shorn of her angles,
pared to a slender carcass, eel, submarine,
then tossed overboard like a surplus torpedo.

On the dock, a thousand triangles are laid out
to shrivel, a distant sun squeezing them dry.
The rest hang from apartment balconies like bunting.

At market, the fins are amber flags, half-mast.
Layered across the stalls like honeycomb,
slabs of gold, manifested greed, parchment, edges.

And finally, the end: a bowl of piss-coloured broth.
The wilted fin floats like ectoplasm, a specimen in
formaldehyde, gelatinous, translucent, barely there.

The pound of flesh is scooped by a spoon.
Brought to the lips, taste is illusive,
but its saltwater tang is strange, familiar.

Beluga

You hang like a stalactite
in the blue, a carved bone,
walrus tusk. Creature of cold,
ethereal, angelic, with the white
curves of a Renaissance maid.
Goddess, I envy your confidence
as you sway towards the glass.
Pale hips, hints of knee joints
sunk into your tail, blubber
in all the right places. No wonder
sailors wrote songs about sirens.
Your milky dome wobbles with the tilt
of your head as you ponder our echoes,
our symphonies. Mercurial, messenger
from a deeper realm, silent as an iceberg,
heavy with cow-like docility. It is mirrored
wonder when your beaked lips form
a gentle bubble in greeting, peering
at us like a child in front of
a television screen.

Whale Fall

Pale jawbones form an archway,
ribs reach into a vaulted ceiling.

No stained glass or frescoes,
only a shattered spinal mosaic:

this is a simple temple
for pilgrims to receive bounty.

Crabs creep from sandy cloisters
to share in the sacrament,

a communion with hammerheads
who tear fraying white flesh

from the chalice of a skull.
They are joined by anglerfish

who carry their candles in the dark:
a vigil for the whale-prophet.

She sank through the centuries
after the hour of her death

to become food-dust in the deep.
This is her afterlife.

Yellow moss clings to the crypt of tail
and squat pectoral fin bones, relics,

headstones, settle with fossil debris
in the sea's vast graveyard.

No choir can be heard in the abyss,
only the silent echoes of humpback hymns.

Eels congregate in empty sockets
and all souls gather for the feast.

Lobsters

Cap Gris Nez, Nord-Pas-De-Calais

Bored with the bilingual chatter between courses,
my sister and I ask to see the lobsters.

We descend a staircase into the cellar;
the encroaching gloom makes us feel like we are
journeying, steadily, to the bottom of the sea.

And there, in a cube of captured saltwater,
is a dark, docile herd. We approach the murky chamber,
dimly lit by an otherworldly glow, like a mothership.

There is something uncomfortably alien about
their long antenna, reaching out for us
as we press our palms against the glass.

Their many legs clack against a sandless seabed.
We are too young to understand that bandaged claws,
clamped, clinical, are not raised in greeting.

The largest, clad in black barding like a war horse,
crawls closer to inspect our blurred faces.
There is a barnacle beauty spot on his hardened cheek.

The others lurk in the shadows, aimless as spiders without webs.
We would like to stay longer, but my uncle is pulling
at our hands, offering an apologetic smile to the indifferent waiter.

My sister wonders aloud at their diet in this small aquarium.
Looking back, it is hard to remember our innocence,
our ignorance of mortality, of consequences.

Bucca

Oldest man of the sea.
Eel-skinned, selkie uncle,
he slithers across an empty beach,
sniffing out the offerings
left by pious fishermen.
Crabs like browned loaves,
the loose change of cockles and clams,
sardines split into silver wings.
He drags them home in a net,
webbed hands slapping at damp sand.
The seaweed on his chin wobbles
with each wet cackle. He flops
through a tide pool and curls himself
into a crevice, clutching at his supper.
It is a simple life: a story of salt and solitude.

Hatchlings

A clutch of ivory grapes in a bowl of sand,
an unguarded fortress of wobbling casements,
popping and peeling themselves in the dark.

Birth is swift, and pale pieces of shell are flimsy armour.

This is what it is to begin life *in media res:*
    the first breath is a scream,
        the first heartbeat, a propeller.

Turtles burst forth from their burials in a flail of flippers.
        There is manic scrabbling as shells scratch
    against each other and they launch down the beach,

        a battlefield in reverse,
            fighting towards the safety of the sea.

Their first steps are a gauntlet,
    a panicked trample,
as they dig into the prints of siblings,

spreading in a splash, black shells glinting
    in the moonlight like spilled oil.

        These tiny tanks crawl in a crazed convoy,
    rattling like pebbles, towards a salty horizon:
a finish line which seems to stretch

                further away
with each frenzied flap.

Shadows float across the sand. Seagulls swoop
low, then drop

like death, lifting wriggling spoils
       into a brightening sky.

Survivors scramble into the shallows. Surging forward,
swallowed by spray, they sink as stones to the depths,
falling from the dawn of the first day.

Valley of the Whales

Wādī al-Ḥītān, Egypt

In the middle of the desert,
there is a strange oasis.
Amongst sandstone pillars
dressed with shells
is the ghost of a lagoon.
A bright bounty
of bones, this dried bowl
provides unexpected fruit,
56 million years in the making.
Whale skeletons have
risen to the surface, once
buried like kings with
trinkets of turtle shells.
The sun disks of their stomachs
reveal a jumble of skulls
smoothed by the wind.
It is an odd afterlife.
The gods of an older pantheon
nose through the dirt,
shedding their earth skin
like serpents. Spines
and ribs carve out
a map scattered
with the memory of salt.
In the middle of the day,
a fennec fox sniffs at fin bones
curled into a foot, then bolts
over a horizon that crackles
and shimmers like water.

Bleaching

Acres of abandoned city,
white ruins cloistered like bare trees
hovering between life and death.
Static, marble held in a museum.

The water is too warm here. Soaking
in a salty broth, the coral is sun-drunk,
starched, broiled. A scale has been
tipped: balance is beyond the reach

of their chalky fingertips. The agony
of snowflake shapes baking in
shallow graves, in blue shadows
which burn and blister and crystalise.

Bright scars left by an algal exodus speak
of the hurt, the masochism of banishment.
This is the collapse of a universe.
A paradise emptied, drained, desecrated.

A lone turtle passes over the dustbowl.
She peers into the pale gloom, tongue clicking
against beaked lips, and then swims, heavily, onward.

Floodplain

The fields are a bowl, filled.
A glacier once scraped out the entrails
of the valley, leaving an oyster shell,
an altar plate ready for silver.

The river bulges
like a dead thing left to the air.
Its mirrored body is burst open:
a hasty gutting. Each pool,
each grey pocket, an amputated scale.
Mallards float on the upturned
belly like pilotfish.

Dry stone walls rise
from the slippery husk, brown and purple,
the exposed veins of a leviathan.

And where the water thickens to mud,
rams stand in the sod, horns curled
into urchins, and observe, unconcerned.

Open gates and fenceposts
gather, shipwrecks in the shallows.
Trees shoulder their broken branches,
masts, crosses, and gesture
in vain towards higher ground.

Two Whale Sharks Collide at the Aquarium

The giant window is lit up like a cinema screen
and a crowd has formed, lapping against the glass.
For a few moments, the water is vast and empty,
just the murky shadow of a manta ray lurking
in the corner of the blue backdrop. And then they arrive.

Two leviathans, loosed from the chariot of Oceanus,
slide silently into view. A scattering of spots
shimmering on each back is a galaxy; stripes stretch
like swimming pool ripples. They are two games
of noughts and crosses drawn in nautical chalk.

These gormless Goliaths float towards each other,
mouths gawping, mirror images, drawing
closer like they are re-enacting a creation myth.
They appear to be gearing up for the gentlest joust
and the spectators gasp, lift phones and cameras,

preparing for the titans to clash. Disaster occurs
in slow motion as their fins brush, but there is no crash,
barely a bump, and then they are curling away,
unfolding from each other in a marine mitosis.

Onlookers cry out despite this anti-climax,
and the combatants retreat, dropped dominoes,
the blue closing over them like a curtain.

Goose Barnacles

I find a crop of tentacles
hissing at low tide.

Their heads curve like snowdrops,
pale shells snapping, splashed
with orange like menstrual rust.

There is something labial
about their beaks, wet tongues
sucking at the rocks.

A crown of pustules, ripe fruit,
making a honking squelch
in the swoop of the wind.

I step closer to inspect
this Medusa mimicry.

The stone face is yours,
and I remember nudging
my nose beneath your jaw,

crawling under you like
a crab and kissing
limpets to your neck,

safe from your gaze
and the storm.

Early Morning Manatee

Recently awakened from slumber
in the shallows, the manatee begins
her dawn grazing. With a softly lumbering
grace, she paddles through the sea grass,
scooping roots to moustache. Grey egg, pebble
smoothed by tides, she is all curves. An easy balloon
animal, she bobs by the shore, snuffling at the bank.
It is a slow life. Peculiar fruit, one wonders on which tree
her silvery flesh grew ripe and furred. Selkie cousin,
she is appropriately named Sirenia. She carries
scars of curiosity: propeller blades have left thin,
pink slices like mouths, kissing across her back,
her flattened fluke, which slaps through
murky water. Despite her long memory,
she has chosen not to bear grudges.
For the world is a bowl, and there
is always more to eat.

Greenland Shark

I was born in the dark, the same year as Shakespeare.
Boundless, with little beauty, I am beyond the philosophies
of heaven and earth, birthed by the metaphysics of the sea.

I am a leviathan. I endure. My bark is equal to my bite:
poison cools in my veins, creates armour from my scales,
although their metal is dulled and holds no light in the deep.

There is a scratch of white beneath my jaw, a bright fork
of flesh torn by an antler, a mark older than electricity.
I gave up my sight long ago, blinded by the pale maggots

who feast on the light from my eyes: I am a forgiving host,
a fish out of time, but I contain an eternity in my bones.
Frost flakes from my fins, finds no resting place on my skin.

The water is cold, but I am a glacier. There are those who
call me Skalugsuak, made from black hair and cloth,
from severed fingers and spite. I am a living relic.

Older than empires and their conquests, I alone am left
unconquered. I am a survivor, and I will survive you.

.

Jellyfish

Abersoch, North Wales

I step further into the dark stretch of sea,
sink until the water forms a cold scarf
under my chin, lift my feet, float:
a satellite to the little village
dipping cobbled toes on the shoreline.

There is something else in orbit.
A gently pulsing moon hovers
in the periphery, an intrusive thought,
a paper phantom, an id.
I know the jellyfish is there,

faceless, barely alive, tendrils spread
like a wedding dress. She is a bulb
of panic, bloated without breath.
The purple calligraphy at her centre
glitters like threads of serotonin.

Neither of us are curious; she does not stray.
Instead, held in uneasy closeness, she is
the window netting I dare not lift, a shower curtain
hiding a knife. Yet, we are kindred in our curves,
twin bodies, quiet souls bobbing in the Styx.

Together in strange symbiosis, I fear I might not
exist if this spectre vanishes. A belt of seaweed
slaps my ankle and it is enough to split the static,
to propel me forward, clutching clumsily at the back
of a grey wave, a poorly-drawn porpoise.

I wade back to the beach, swampish, pimpled,
pulling wet strands of hair from my throat.
There is a blubbery shipwreck melting into the sand.
I pause, consider the twist of wounds within the carcass,
then continue to my towel, blown to a dome by the wind.

Ghosting

An iceberg of green netting floats
in the open ocean. Unmelting, its ropes
sway like jellyfish tendrils, a forest
of hardened kelp. A swell lifts
the decaying veil, then drops it again,
a terrible shroud.

A spinner dolphin hangs
in suspended animation,
eyes black as mussels' shells,
fins holding up knotted chains,
Marley's ghost, snared harbinger.

The web reaches sandwards
to where it is anchored by lobster cages
piled like sunken aviaries, their yellow lichen
glinting with the hidden light of fool's gold.

Abandoned crab traps are still making a catch,
set by long-dead fishermen whose boats rust in the bay.
Summoned by curiosity, they crawl over the coins of shells,
the burial ground of their brothers. A chorus of ghostly clacking
goes unheeded. They do not turn back.

A seal swirls through the blue murk,
considers an easy snack, but can sense a death
it does not bring, fears the noose, the macabre collage:

a turtle shell weighing down the gauze like a cannon ball,
a hammerhead who came to scavenge, but sprang the trap.

They are caught, collateral, an afterthought.

The Loneliness of the Long Distance Waddler

Scientists have been left baffled by this
minimalist tableau: a vast, empty canvas
and one small inkblot in the corner
like a scribbled signature.

A lone penguin, empty-handed ambler,
is journeying northwards, away from the colony.
Her movements have the certainty of a sprinter;
her staunch toddle is direct, determined.

Broad triangles of webbed footprints form
an arrow in the snow. The destination in unknown,
but her beak points towards mountains, slumped
like the snoozing lumps of elephant seals.

She is swift in her retreat from the black splash
where the blimps of a thousand bodies bob together:
so much jostling, the gakker of a never-ending gathering.
Perhaps she is searching for quiet on the quietest continent.

Monochromatic philosopher, venturing further into white noise.
She is a satellite, she is Captain Oates, she is an escaped shadow.
World-weary, but persisting in her path without struggle,
towards the soft nothingness of the horizon.

Consider the Selkie

I sink into the steaming water,
wrap it around me like a coat.
The tub follows my curves,
holds me close, enamel mermaid purse.
A shower wouldn't satisfy:
I need to wear water like a skin.
It is a process, learning
to like this body, its ripples
and roundness. The way
my thighs press into
the smooth arms of the bath.
But then I consider the selkie.

Almost-more-than siren
and her blubber, the folds
of her soft belly, bursting
from seal slip. Perhaps this
is why I am fond of the water,
the way its cloth clings to
my nakedness: I feel less raw,
unexposed. It is a journey,
but maybe, after this soaking,
I will slow down in front of the mirror
and stop searching for another skin.

Sand Tiger Sharks at the Frying Pan Tower

Thirty-four miles off the coast of Cape Fear,
the water is a grey waiting room.

Blurred stilts of the once great tower
stand like the pillars of an abandoned temple.

The kelpish sway of a dawn-coloured sea
is deceptive: this is a place of stasis.

Out of the murk, strange shapes appear,
barely swimming. Elongated blimps

the colour of nails, of the pipes in the seabed.

A herd of sand tiger sharks gathers,
docile as cattle, to enjoy the ebb and flow.

Their scales flash gold, coins at the bottom
of a fountain, leftover ammunition.

Unblinking eyes, like the dead, swivel
across the fog, glimpse rays swooping below.

Suspended in the clash of currents, specimens
in formaldehyde. It is a comfortable purgatory.

Tide Pool

This cupped palm of sea
is a micro-cosmos.

A swirl of kelpy nebula,
barnacles like comets,

their tails made of sunlight
sparkling on small waves.

An ocean in miniature,
like a bottle, a glitter globe,

a cauldron of primordial broth.
An egg case, hardened

womb, parcel without postage,
shaped like a manta ray shadow.

Shipwrecks of shells, fossil dust.
The pool is both graveyard and nursery.

Crabs snap at the fish circling
like aquarium sharks, and escape

the ebb and flow, tidal nomads.
Beached anemones bleed and clot,

and all the semi-submerged must wait,
for any drop could become a flood.

My Father Eating Mussels

Skipton, North Yorkshire

Miles and miles from the sea,
an unbroken yolk cools within
the black, salt-dusted shell
of the strange egg held between
my father's thumb and forefinger.

With the ease of an expert,
he uses another shell, clacking
like a beak, to tear orange flesh
from its dark cradle, a vulture
picking over another's corpse.

This act of cannibalism
occurs in mid-air over a basin
of yellow broth and inky rocks.
Discarded shells, empty as coffins,
sink into the soup, opening like wings.

The smell of tide pools, of seasonal cafés,
stretches across the table. It has been
a long time since we sat together,
scratchy with sand, shivering like seaweed,
on the front by the beach at Wimereux.

Thresher Shark

A flash of dagger
through blue breakers.
Sea mesh splits
beneath the gull.
Lash of tailfin,
splash of feathers,
tossed upwards
by shark,
stranger bird.
Twist of glass,
clash suspended, duet.
Thrash of prey,
jaws clamp
on bright cross,
spray, struggle.
Success. They crash
down like a wreck,
gush of red
and shredded flesh.
Carcass bobs
on foam-sweat,
then water stretches
over shadow,
sated threat.

Walrussey

For Wally

They say that you dozed off on an iceberg
and awoke on Irish shores, a Nordic visitor
without a horde, lonely wanderer, far
from your arctic home. Child of ice mountains,
you have ridden these Celtic currents
for months, travelling south, strange sun-pilgrim.
They say that you are lost, gorging yourself
on Cornish clams, preparing for a return journey,
but your continental visits are inscrutable.
Fingertip of Nuliajuk, you bask on beaches
like the discarded glove of an old god,
with your leathery hide, you are your own luggage.
Seafarer, you did not pack light for your odyssey.
Rolling in the snowflakes of the seafoam,
you nose boulders with grizzled whiskers,
snuggle into rocky crevices, coldsick, exiled,
missing the sounds and smells of the herd.
They say that you came to the harbour seeking company.
At night you bob among boats, mourning your lost brothers,
and watch the stars in a black sky, wishing for
a green, kelpy flicker of the aurora borealis.
Perhaps you are a scout from a melting world,
a tusked omen, disaster warning. Dear walrus
of wanderlust, moustachioed philosopher,
you are all of us, floating in an ocean-universe,
with no choice but to go on seeking.

Mola mola

Ocean sunfish, strangely named,
for you are clearly lunar. Even your
binomial nomenclature, from 'millstone',
seems a linguistic joke, when I watch
your round body, moon reflection,

breaking the surface, bobbing
like a life raft, a parasite picnic
for weary sea birds and scavengers.
I wonder, planisphere *poisson*,
what you would call yourself.

Wanderer of the open whale road,
monument, paving stone,
not everyone can understand
the grace of the already-assembled,
the solitary swimmer who is
floating, not drowning.

You are the lost frisbee of giants,
two large triangle fins like a prank.
Unassuming and unmatched,
a circle of bone, half-moving itself
across the Atlantic. Customer of currents,
baffler of taxidermists, beacon, meteorite.

You are a solar panel, recharging,
a bright idea, ready for the deep dive.
As tall as you are wide, mathematically
pleased with your own symmetry.

And your mass contains multitudes:
with 300 million offspring, creator goddess,
you release a haze of star-shaped fry
like a galaxy giving birth to itself.

Lion's Mane Jellyfish

Somewhere, in this vast galaxy
of salt and water, there is a nebula.
Clouds of orange and red twist
within a dome that shimmers
in the coastal sunlight.

The jellyfish blooms like
a mushroom cloud: an explosion
frozen in formaldehyde. No roar,
no jaws, but a crown of golden
tentacles, trailing anchors.

She is a pomegranate, squeezed,
bursting with bloodless innards,
tendrils curling into a labyrinth.
Minotaur, monster, carrying
her own stinging fences.

A ghost at the banquet table,
soft iceberg, swelling like linen
thrown overboard, like desperation.
She is her own heart, thumping
silently, carving out an ocean.

There is a scuba diver,
approaching cautiously with
camera raised to our Chimera.
She hovers like a mothership,
eerie, edged with green.

First contact is brief, wordless,
then the alien retreats into the blue.
She continues her solitary journey
along the current, underwater aurora,
shivering with her own light.

Ichthyosaur Fossil at the Natural History Museum

It is a stone snapshot of tragedy behind glass,
held within the polished wood of a picture frame.
A memory of death carved out of the earth.

Her long beak is closed, gritted pain: she did not cry out
in the final moments, although the one visible eye bulges,
planetary, a steel moon full of fatal knowledge.

There is a jumble of tiny bones, trinkets, treasure,
held behind a cage of long slender bones, the comb of her ribs
keeping them safe, beside the faint dip of her heart.

One flipper is pressed to her belly, soothing them all.
Each individual scale has been preserved, locked
together in chainmail, like bubbles of grey coral.

And her daughter, mirror image, sharer of fate.
She was born tail-first, died nosing at her mother,
forever joined in this fossilised afterlife.

187 million years of mothers and daughters since,
and still we carry life and death, always, with us.

Requiem for a Great White Shark in Formaldehyde

When the anxiety rises from unsettling depths,
I don't force myself to picture a tropical beach
or gently bubbling stream. Instead, I walk
through the rubble of an abandoned wildlife park
somewhere in South-Eastern Australia.

The nets of metal fences creak in a light wind,
litter flutters like birds, but nothing living is left.
It is a dystopian scene and I cross the threshold,
solitary, survivor. Beyond the gift shop,
the dried-up penguin pool, the rotting
botanical garden, there is a purposefully
built room which houses a tank.

I slowly approach the glass, and out
of the green gloom appears a wraith,
the black zigzag of jaws like a beartrap.
Her name is Rosie, a Great White caught
in tuna nets the year I turned six, and didn't
know the word to explain that I was afraid
of small spaces.

                Now she is caught again,
suspended in formaldehyde like a lab specimen,
like an embryo. Her muddy skin is time-shrunken
leather, tightened over pale gums, creased around
unblinking eyes that find me in the dark.

A drooping fin breaks the surface of a gradually

descending waterline: a film prop, our planet
in chemical microcosm. Her belly is stitched
from the necropsy that proved her innocence.
The scar shimmers like a wave in the yellowy light
of water which has never seen salt or seaweed.

This is a strange afterlife, but I am glad we have
found each other. I press my fingertips
to the cold, flat walls of her cage, breathe
carefully against the prickling at my neck.
When the anxiety rises from unsettling depths,
I visit Rosie in all her still, soupy immortality,
and remember what it means to float.

Blue Lobster

Fishermen haul lobster pots
from grey waves, dragging currency
from a bottomless fountain.

Aviaries shivering with bronze moss
clatter against the boat, weighted
with a jumble of black pebbles.

Cages are thrown open, emptied,
and a chattering crowd, flapping like crows,
spills as oil-slick into plastic crates.

There is a gift. The sea has shed a part of itself.
Flash of fluorescence, blooming like a bruise.
A blue lobster, one in two million.

She is sea glass, sapphire, rough-cut
mosaic tile, glittering like a ghost, lifted
with a reverence reserved for the rare.

There is a quick, clumsy gathering,
the click of a camera, then she is returned
to the sea, dropped like a coin, like a wish.

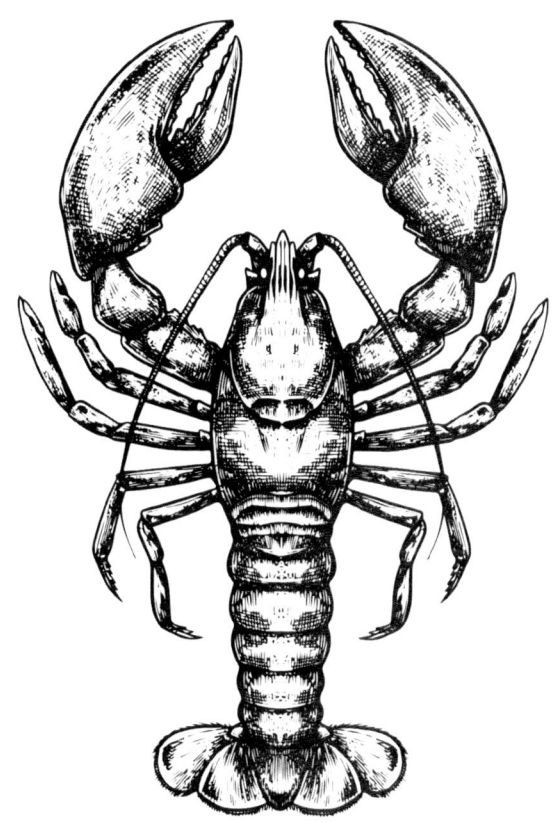

Acknowledgements

Acknowledgements are due to the editors of the following publications in which some of these poems first appeared:

Typehouse Literary Magazine, The Coachella Review, Atrium, Okay Donkey, Boats Against the Current, Olney Magazine, Paddler Press, Green Ink Poetry, IceFloe Press, Canary, Olit, Seaborne Magazine, Heavy Feather Review, Visual Verse, Juniper, Fahmidan Journal.

www.blackcatpress.co.uk